FLYING
JUST PLANE FUN

Julie Grist

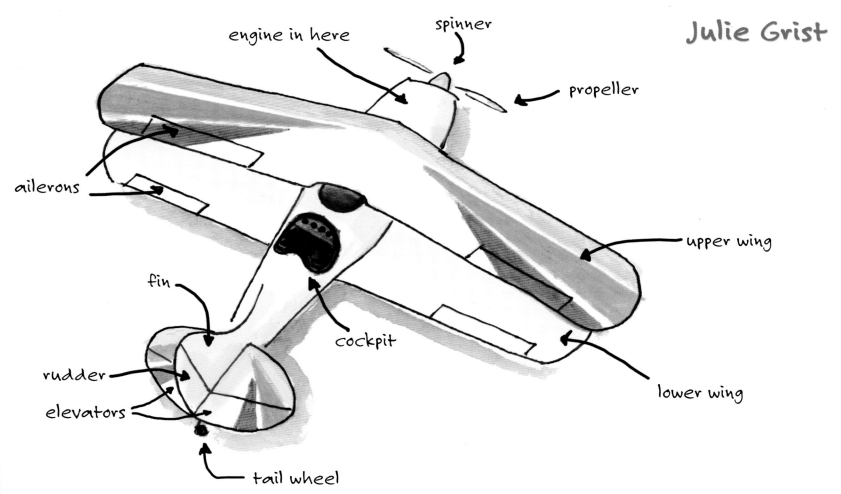

engine in here

spinner

propeller

ailerons

upper wing

fin

cockpit

rudder

elevators

lower wing

tail wheel

Los Angeles, CA

FLIGHT PLAN

FOR DAD WITH LOVE

AIRCRAFT IDENTIFICATION	AIRCRAFT TYPE	
N444PR	STEEN SKYBOLT: OPEN COCKPIT, TWO-SEATER BIPLANE	

AIRCRAFT COLOR	TRUE AIRSPEED	CRUISING ALTITUDE
WHITE AND YELLOW	125 MPH	1500 FEET

DEPARTURE POINT	DEPARTURE TIME	EST. TIME EN ROUTE
WAUPACA, WISCONSIN	9:30 AM	1:12 HOURS (INCLUDING DONUT STOP!)

DESTINATION		NUMBER ABOARD
OMRO, WISCONSIN	ONE GRANDPA ONE GRANDSON →	2

Spoonbender Books
419 N. Larchmont Blvd., #4
Los Angeles, CA 90004
www.spoonbenderbooks.com

Publisher's Cataloging-in-Publication
(Provided by Quality Books, Inc.)

Grist, Julie.
  Flying : Just Plane Fun / written and illustrated by Julie Grist. -- 1st paperback ed.
  p. cm.
  SUMMARY: A young boy flies in his grandfather's home-built biplane over the Wisconsin countryside in this introduction to the basics of aviation and the joy of being airborne.
  Audience: Ages 5-12.
  LCCN 2002095012
  ISBN 0-9725750-2-2

  1. Flight--Juvenile literature. 2. Aeronautics--Juvenile literature. 3. Airplanes, Home-built--Juvenile literature. 4. Biplanes--Juvenile literature. 5. Grandparent and child--Juvenile literature. [1. Flight. 2. Aeronautics. 3. Airplanes, Home-built. 4. Biplanes.   5. Grandparents.]   I. Title.

TL547.G75 2003   629.13
                        QB133-996

-Printed in China-

Dear Flyboy,

Congratulations on your first flight! This is a logbook of our day in the skies together over Wisconsin. With a little more stick time, you could be a real fine flyer.

Love, Gramps

ROLL OUT

Hangar →

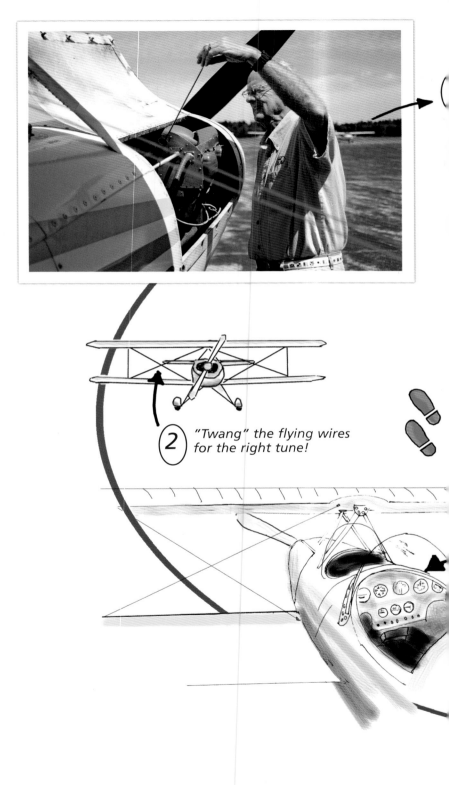

2 "Twang" the flying wires for the right tune!

Let's roll my homebuilt airplane out of the hangar for inspection. If there is anything not working properly I want to find out while on the ground – not in the air! Every pilot does a "walk around" of the plane before climbing aboard. Find #1 and begin the preflight inspection.

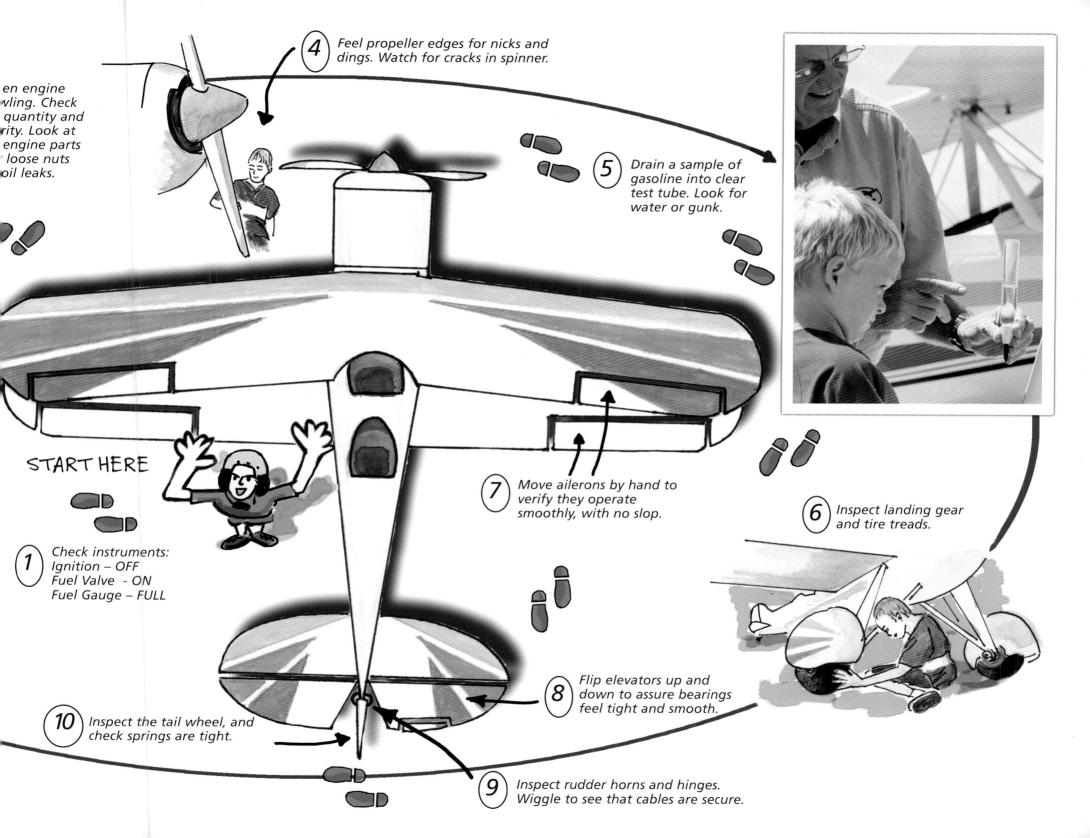

4 Feel propeller edges for nicks and dings. Watch for cracks in spinner.

en engine wling. Check quantity and rity. Look at engine parts loose nuts oil leaks.

5 Drain a sample of gasoline into clear test tube. Look for water or gunk.

START HERE

7 Move ailerons by hand to verify they operate smoothly, with no slop.

6 Inspect landing gear and tire treads.

1 Check instruments:
Ignition – OFF
Fuel Valve - ON
Fuel Gauge – FULL

8 Flip elevators up and down to assure bearings feel tight and smooth.

10 Inspect the tail wheel, and check springs are tight.

9 Inspect rudder horns and hinges. Wiggle to see that cables are secure.

ON THE RAMP

Now it's time to climb in and make some noise. Hoist yourself into the copilot's seat. Buckle up the seat and shoulder belts. I don't want you to fall out!

We strap on intercom HEADSET RADIOS so we can talk to one another and the airport TOWER. I set our radio to 122.8, the aviation frequency.

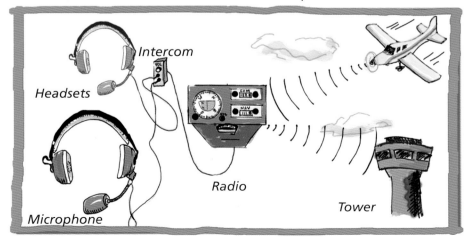

Intercom

Headsets

Radio

Tower

Microphone

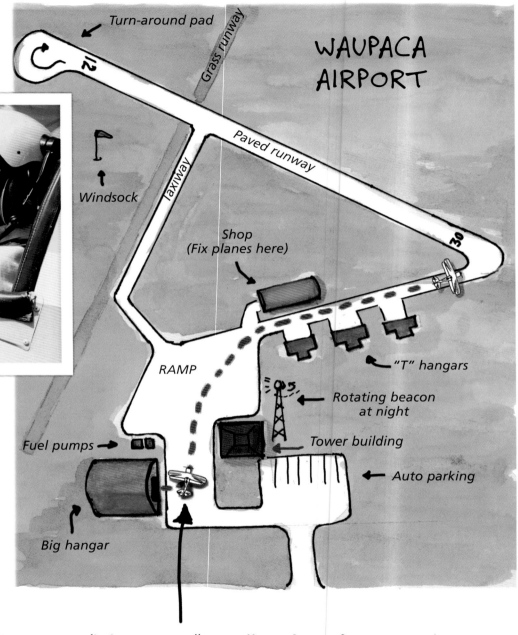

WAUPACA AIRPORT

Turn-around pad

12

Grass runway

Paved runway

Taxiway

Windsock

Shop (Fix planes here)

RAMP

"T" hangars

30

Rotating beacon at night

Fuel pumps

Tower building

Big hangar

Auto parking

"Clear prop" I call before firing up the engine to alert all to stand clear. The 180 horsepower four-banger roars to life. We taxi slowly across the ramp toward the runway.

Holding short of runway three zero we run through our checklist. Here it's color-coded to the arrows in the cockpit.

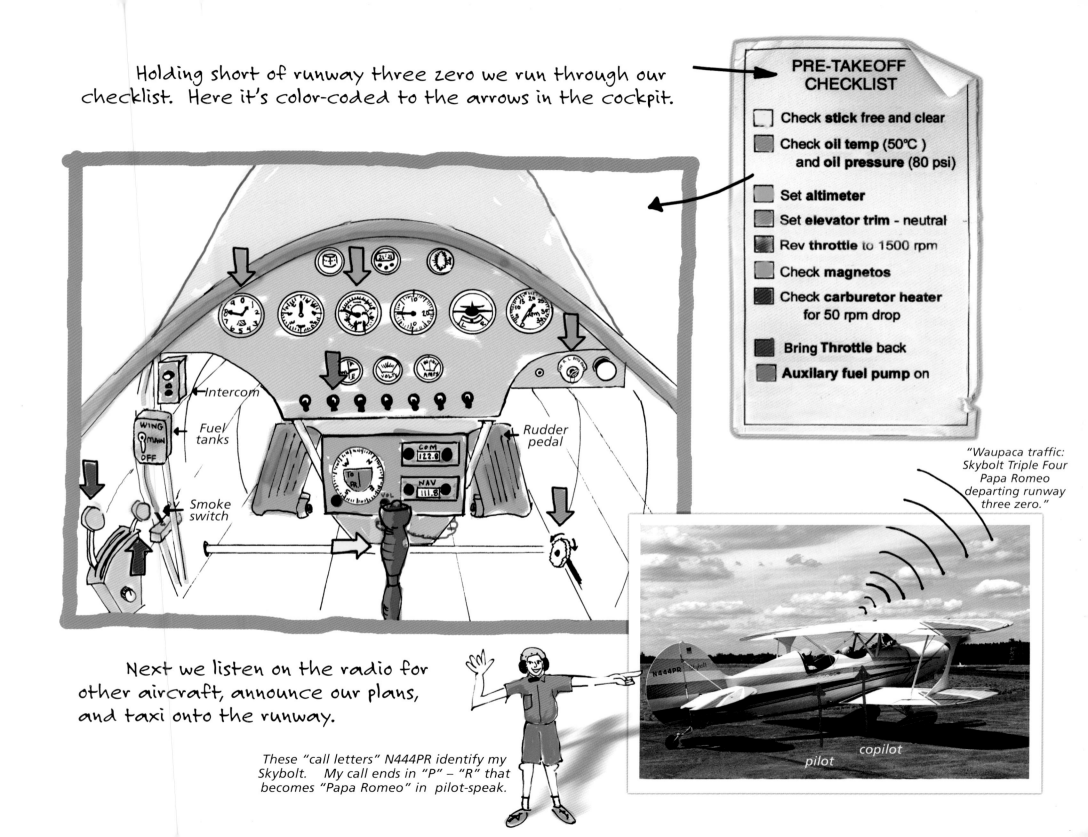

PRE-TAKEOFF CHECKLIST

☐ Check **stick** free and clear

☐ Check **oil temp** (50°C) and **oil pressure** (80 psi)

☐ Set **altimeter**

☐ Set **elevator trim** – neutral

☐ Rev **throttle** to 1500 rpm

☐ Check **magnetos**

☐ Check **carburetor heater** for 50 rpm drop

☐ Bring **Throttle** back

☐ **Auxilary fuel pump** on

Intercom

Fuel tanks

Smoke switch

Rudder pedal

COM 122.8

NAV 111.8

"Waupaca traffic: Skybolt Triple Four Papa Romeo departing runway three zero."

Next we listen on the radio for other aircraft, announce our plans, and taxi onto the runway.

These "call letters" N444PR identify my Skybolt. My call ends in "P" – "R" that becomes "Papa Romeo" in pilot-speak.

pilot   copilot

TAKEOFF!

I ease the throttle forward, the engine revs up, and the plane races ahead. My feet dance back and forth on the rudder pedals, keeping our nose pointed straight down the runway.

At 90 miles per hour, I gently pull back on the stick and the wheels leave the ground.

We're flying!

Say cheese!

The vertical speed indicator shows our rate of ascent or descent. Here we're climbing at 400 feet per minute.

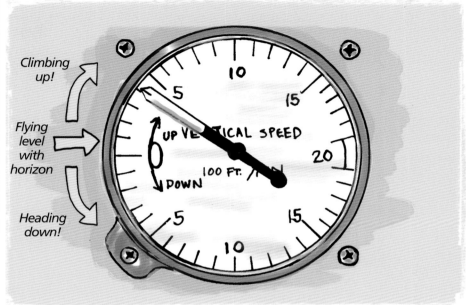

Climbing up!

Flying level with horizon

Heading down!

UP VERTICAL SPEED

DOWN

100 FT.

The airspeed indicator shows our speed in miles per hour.

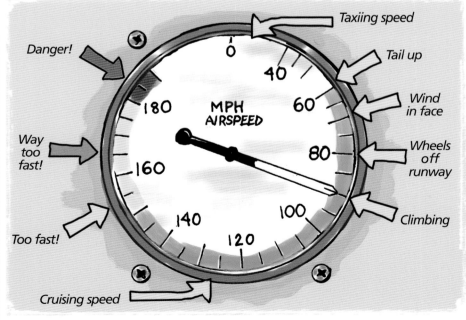

Danger!

Way too fast!

Too fast!

Cruising speed

MPH AIRSPEED

Taxiing speed

Tail up

Wind in face

Wheels off runway

Climbing

AIRBORNE!

I love it up here!

Do you know how flight works? It has to do with four key elements: LIFT, WEIGHT, THRUST and DRAG.

LIFT is produced by air flowing over the curved surface of a wing. We need lift to overcome our WEIGHT. The Skybolt is packed with a heavy engine, fuel, seats, instruments, and a "turtledeck" compartment for extra stuff. Plus the weight of you and me and all the ice cream we ate yesterday!

We use the THRUST of the engine and propeller to overcome the DRAG of our big body mass moving through the air.

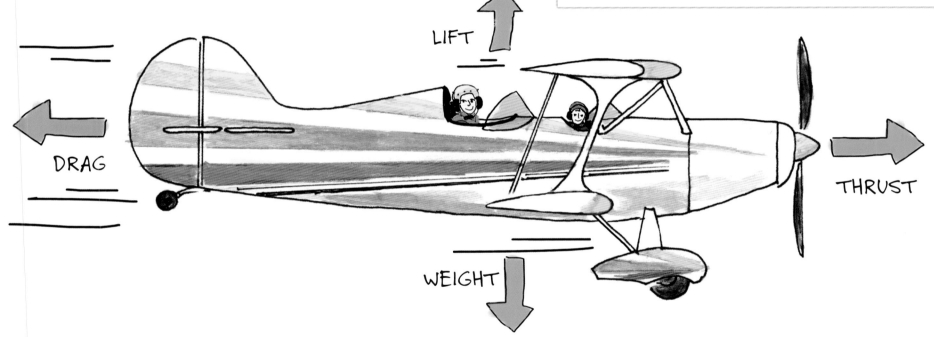

LIFT

DRAG

THRUST

WEIGHT

LIFT

lower pressure

wing

Air molecules passing over the curved top of the wing must travel a longer distance. They get spread apart and this creates lower pressure.

Air molecules flowing on the under side of the wing take the easier straight route, staying shoulder-to-shoulder strong. They push upward against the lower pressure of the weaklings above, and this provides the lift that keeps planes aloft.

CONTROLS

I use the STICK and RUDDER PEDALS to control the plane. The STICK operates two things: the AILERONS, which tip us into a turn, and the ELEVATORS, which let us climb and dive.

The PEDALS control the RUDDER which steers our nose in the direction we want to go. Hands and feet work in unison to fly the Skybolt "smooth and clean."

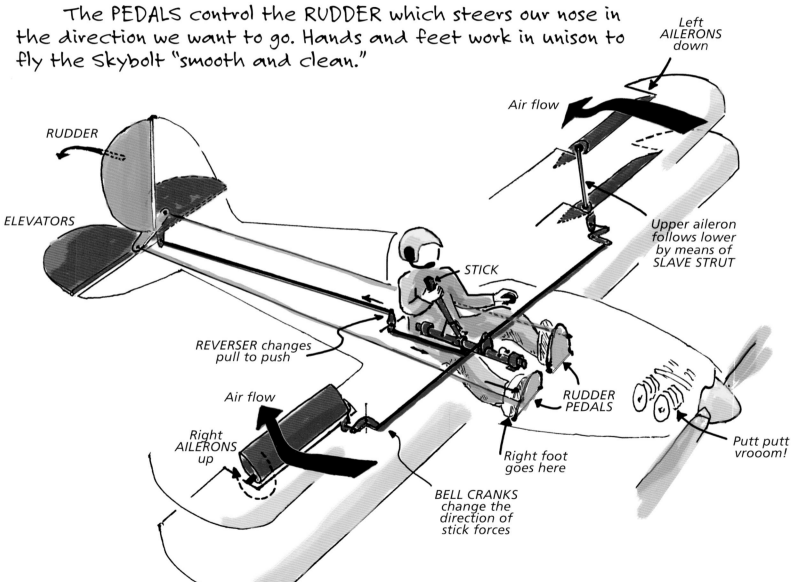

RUDDER

ELEVATORS

Air flow

Left AILERONS down

STICK

Upper aileron follows lower by means of SLAVE STRUT

REVERSER changes pull to push

Air flow

Right AILERONS up

RUDDER PEDALS

Right foot goes here

Putt putt vrooom!

BELL CRANKS change the direction of stick forces

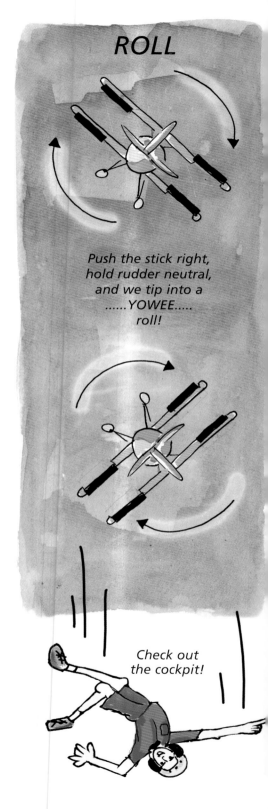

ROLL

Push the stick right, hold rudder neutral, and we tip into a ......YOWEE..... roll!

Check out the cockpit!

COCKPIT

The ALTIMETER shows our height above sea level. Here you see we're flying at about 2500 feet.

Keep your eyes moving - scanning the skies and the instruments.

The CHRONOMETER tells us our flight time in the air.

VERTICAL SPEED INDICATOR

The AIR SPEED INDICATOR shows we're cruising at 125 miles per hour.

The radio PUSH-TO-TALK button is on stick.

The TURN COORDINATOR shows our relationship to the real horizon. We're in a right turn here to avoid that pile of cumulus clouds ahead!

Pulling back on the STICK moves the plane elevators up, and we climb.

Pushing the STICK forward we dive. Tickle tummy!

NAVIGATION

I love flying over the Wisconsin countryside. I know my way around just by looking down at the rivers, highways and barns that are so familiar. I fly these skies a lot.

When we're flying somewhere new, we have to use NAVIGATIONAL tools to figure out where we are and where we're headed.

First, we need to use a basic compass and learn to speak about direction in degrees. We say we're headed "southeast at 130 degrees" instead of just saying "heading south."

Can you follow our flight route on the AERONAUTICAL CHART I've clipped here?

1. Take off from Waupaca, heading southwest at 200 degrees toward Saxeville.

2. Change heading to 130 degrees southeast.

3. Touch down at farm for fly-in breakfast.

4. Head 3. degree northwes toward hom

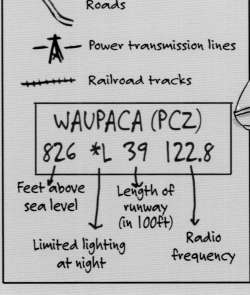

LEGEND

Airports having Control Towers shown in blue, all others magenta.

⬤❘	⊗	Hard surfaced runways 1500 ft to 8069 ft long
⬤❘	✚	Hard surfaced runways greater than 8069 ft
⬤	◯	Grass air strips
Ⓡ		Restricted: Private runway Emergency landing only
▲		Obstruction 1000 ft and higher
⌃		Obstruction below 1000 ft
∿		Roads
⟍⚡⟍		Power transmission lines
┼┼┼┼┼┼		Railroad tracks

WAUPACA (PCZ)
826 *L 39 122.8

Feet above sea level

Limited lighting at night

Length of runway (in 100ft)

Radio frequency

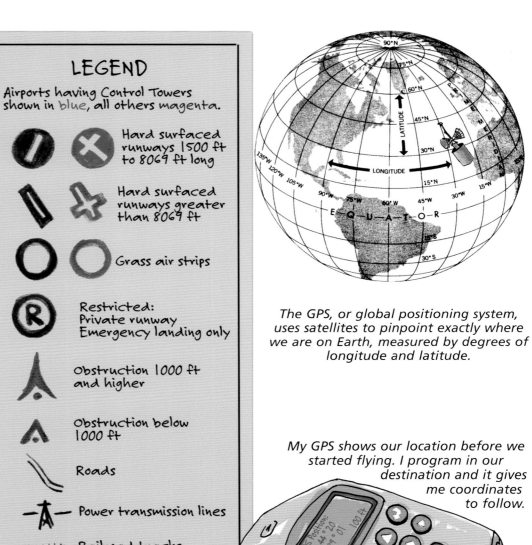

The GPS, or global positioning system, uses satellites to pinpoint exactly where we are on Earth, measured by degrees of longitude and latitude.

My GPS shows our location before we started flying. I program in our destination and it gives me coordinates to follow.

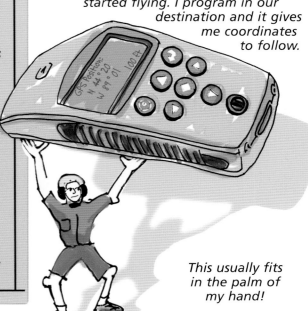

This usually fits in the palm of my hand!

FLY-IN

Next we touch down for a fly-in breakfast at Munsil Williams' farm near Omro. I love landing on his 1500 foot grass strip nestled in between Highway 44 and his silver hangar. Fly-ins take place at small airfields all across the country on summer days.

Many of these guys built their own planes. We love to talk shop, compare horsepower, and tell flying tales.

Cows in here
Workshop
Hangar
Grass strip
Highway 44

Munsil, our host, is an active "Flying Farmer." He's building a Vans RV-8 aluminum airplane in his workshop.

Les has been flying for 36 years.

Leroy flies a high-wing Ultralight he built himself.

You know this geek!

Norm flies a Piper C[ub] on floats, wheels a[nd] skis. He's built two biplanes and restore[d] old planes.

Bill won so many air races that his plane, called "Buster" is in the Smithsonian Institute in Washington D.C.

Jack flew a P-51 Mustang in World War II. He owns 27 planes, including a Grumman Mallard, a Turbine Goose, and a Saberliner Jet.

Jim builds model airplanes. He's great with a scroll saw!

Each year about 12,000 small aircraft fly into Oshkosh, Wisconsin, for the EAA Fly-In. I love to line up in the sky with dozens of other planes. It's so busy we come in and land at about one plane every twenty seconds!

There are plenty of homebuilt planes and vintage birds on display, as well as thrilling aerobatic shows to watch in the sky. Check out the wing walker.

Pilots pitch tents under their wings and stay for days to revel in all things aviation. Let's camp out under the Skybolt next summer.

Hanging ten in mid-air!

E POST~ENT

EAA takes thousands under its wing

Experimental Aircraft Association draws 500,000 fans to Oshkosh

50c

For kids who want to fly.

YOUNG EAGLES

EAA

BUILDING A PLANE

As a young boy, I always dreamed of flying. I drew this picture for my dad when I was just ten years old, right after my first ride in an airplane.

alum ch...

35

15"

21

Piper PA-22 nose cowling or equiv.

COWLING DETAILS

FROM JIM TO FATHER

I built and flew radio-controlled model airplanes and came to know I could construct a full size plane.

WING SPAN, UPPER	24 ft
WING SPAN, LOWER	23 ft
LENGTH	19 ft
HEIGHT	7 ft
GROSS WEIGHT	1650
EMPTY WEIGHT	1080
WING LOADING	11 lb/s

STEEN SKYBOLT

The Skybolt was designed by a man named La Mar Steen who hand-drew the plans on fourteen large pages such as this one.

Dropping fuel tank into fuselage.

Will it fit together?

Covering wing ribs with fabric.

*I know every
nut and bolt
of this bird!*

It took me eight years to build the Skybolt. I began building in the basement and eventually moved to the garage. I spent every spare minute working on it. Your grandma was great to put up with my plane and me!

The Skybolt is constructed of steel tubing, wood and fabric. I needed to measure, saw, weld, bolt, sew and wire many different components.

I was so thrilled the first time we "ran up" the engine. My dream was really coming true!

AEROBATICS

When airplanes perform stunt maneuvers such as rolls and loops we call it AEROBATICS. Some people call it crazy, some call it fun. I call it an essential to good flying.

A pilot who knows the strengths and limits of a plane will have better control in adverse situations, and will be a smooth and confident flyer. At least that's what I tell your grandma when I'm waltzing around in the skies!

THE SLOW ROLL

View of the horizon in a shallow left turn.

View of the horizon in a steep banked turn.

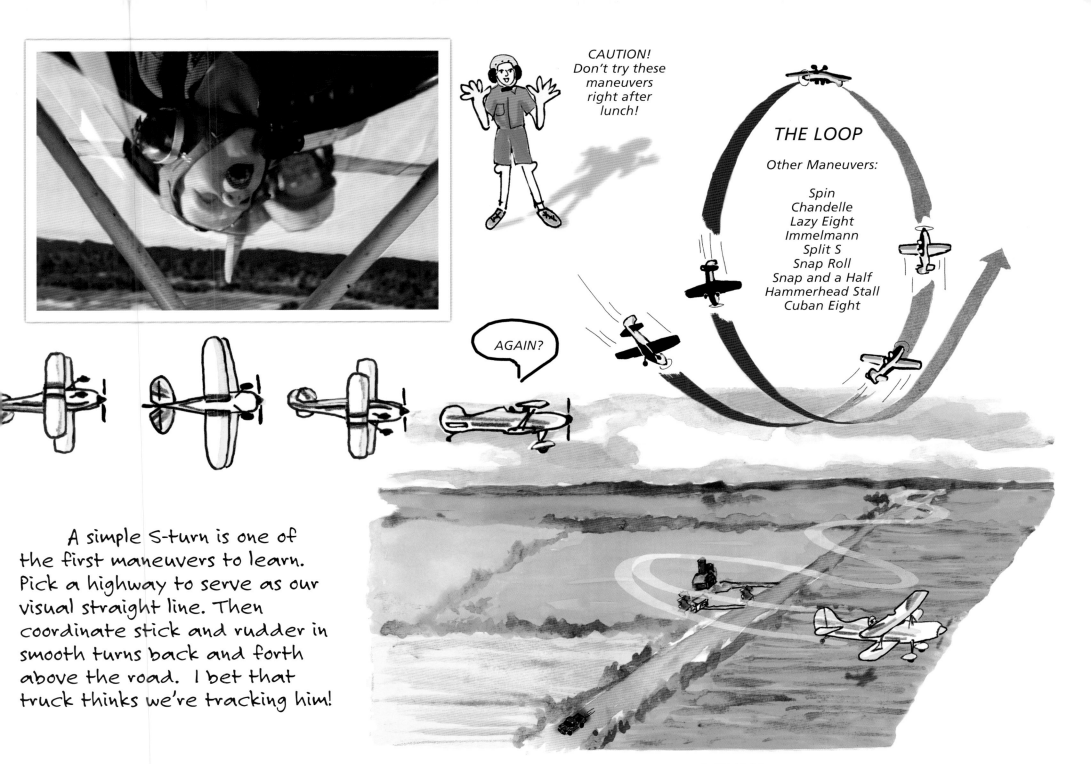

CAUTION!
Don't try these maneuvers right after lunch!

THE LOOP

Other Maneuvers:

Spin
Chandelle
Lazy Eight
Immelmann
Split S
Snap Roll
Snap and a Half
Hammerhead Stall
Cuban Eight

AGAIN?

A simple S-turn is one of the first maneuvers to learn. Pick a highway to serve as our visual straight line. Then coordinate stick and rudder in smooth turns back and forth above the road. I bet that truck thinks we're tracking him!

THE S-TURN

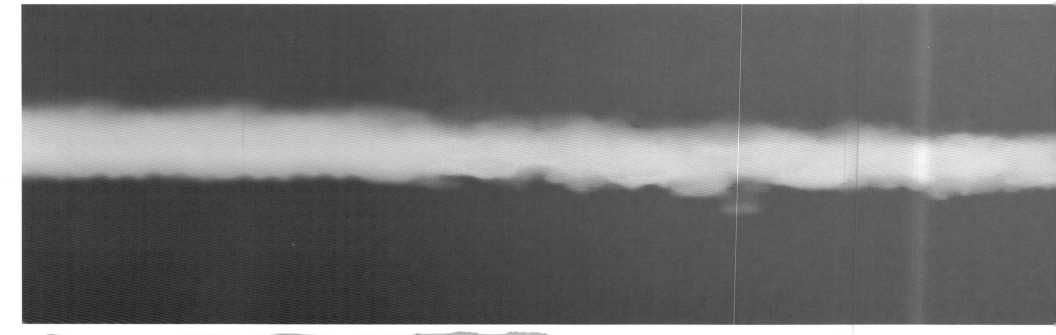

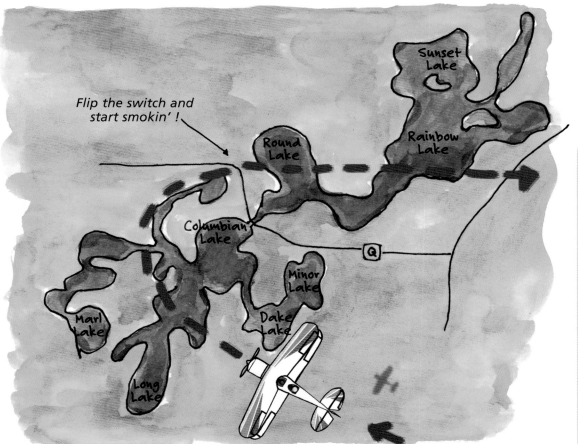

Flip the switch and start smokin'!

Sunset Lake

Rainbow Lake

Round Lake

Columbian Lake

Q

Minor Lake

Dake Lake

Marl Lake

Long Lake

Before we head back to the airport, let's buzz over the Chain O'Lakes and smoke the kids on the dock. I rigged this smoker just to show off!

LANDING

We're on approach for runway three zero, coming in from the west. Help me scan the skies and radio for other aircraft, then we'll drop into the proper landing pattern.

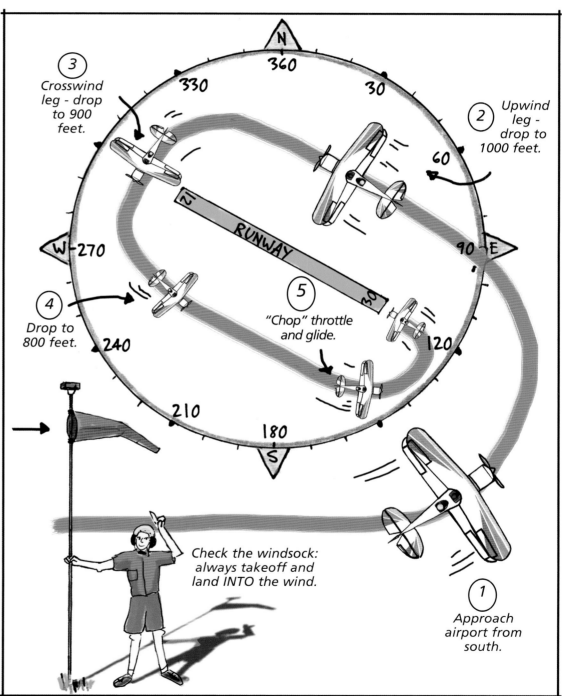

3 Crosswind leg - drop to 900 feet.

2 Upwind leg - drop to 1000 feet.

4 Drop to 800 feet.

5 "Chop" throttle and glide.

RUNWAY

Check the windsock: always takeoff and land INTO the wind.

1 Approach airport from south.

We touch down nice and easy at home base once again, and taxi back to the ramp. Time to refuel, stow our helmets, and push the plane back into the hangar.

Congratulations on your first trip as copilot! I hope we can take to the skies together again soon. Some day you too could be a pilot.

xxxooo
Gramps

This is to certify that my grandson flew as copilot in the Skybolt N444PR on a clear fine day thereby successfully completing an aeronautic tour of central Wisconsin. Hope you continue your training!

GRAMPS' SEAL of APPROVAL